100
Drawing Promps
for
Animal Lovers

Includes a list of 100 animals
and
a variety of frames to draw them in.

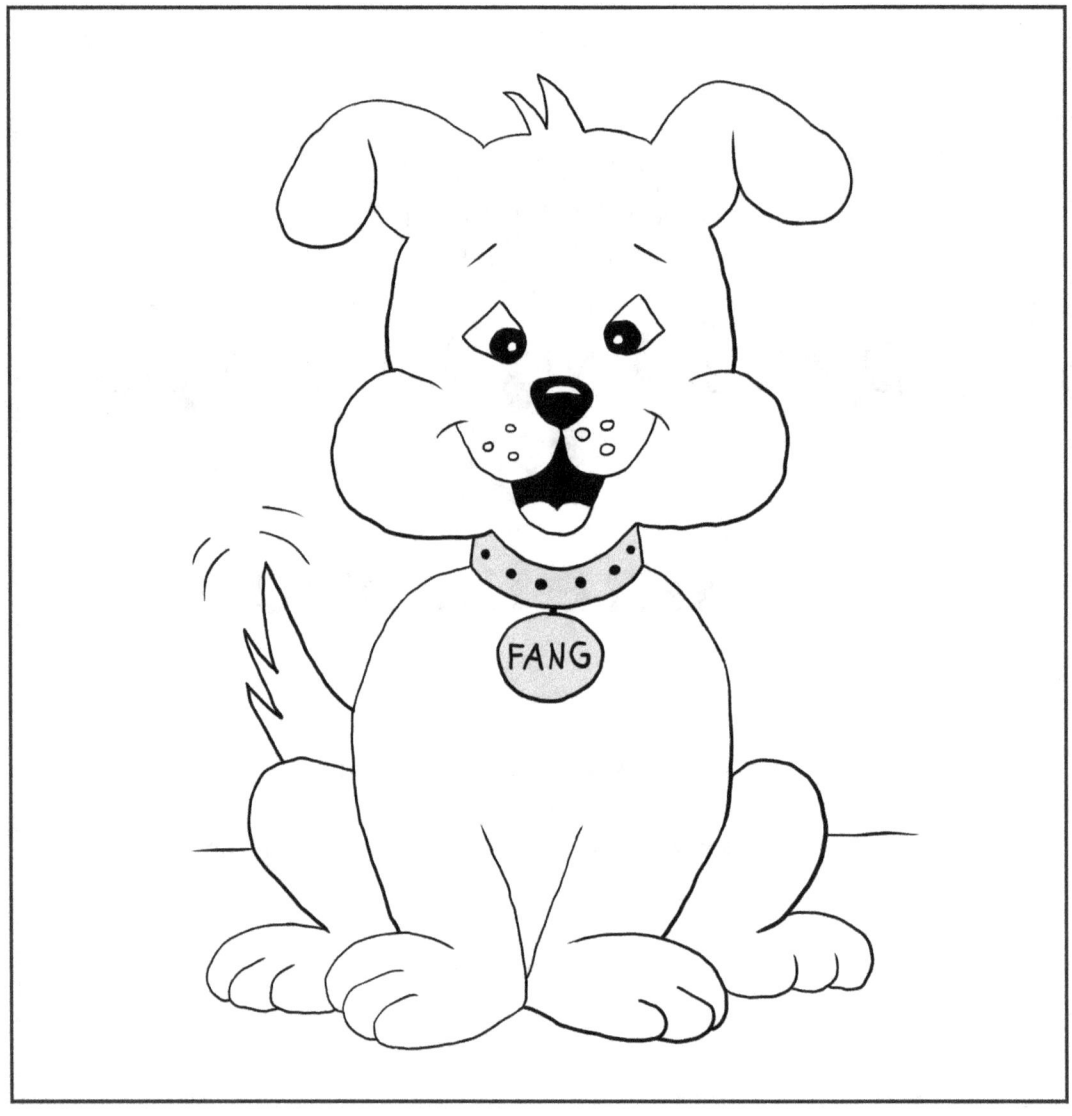

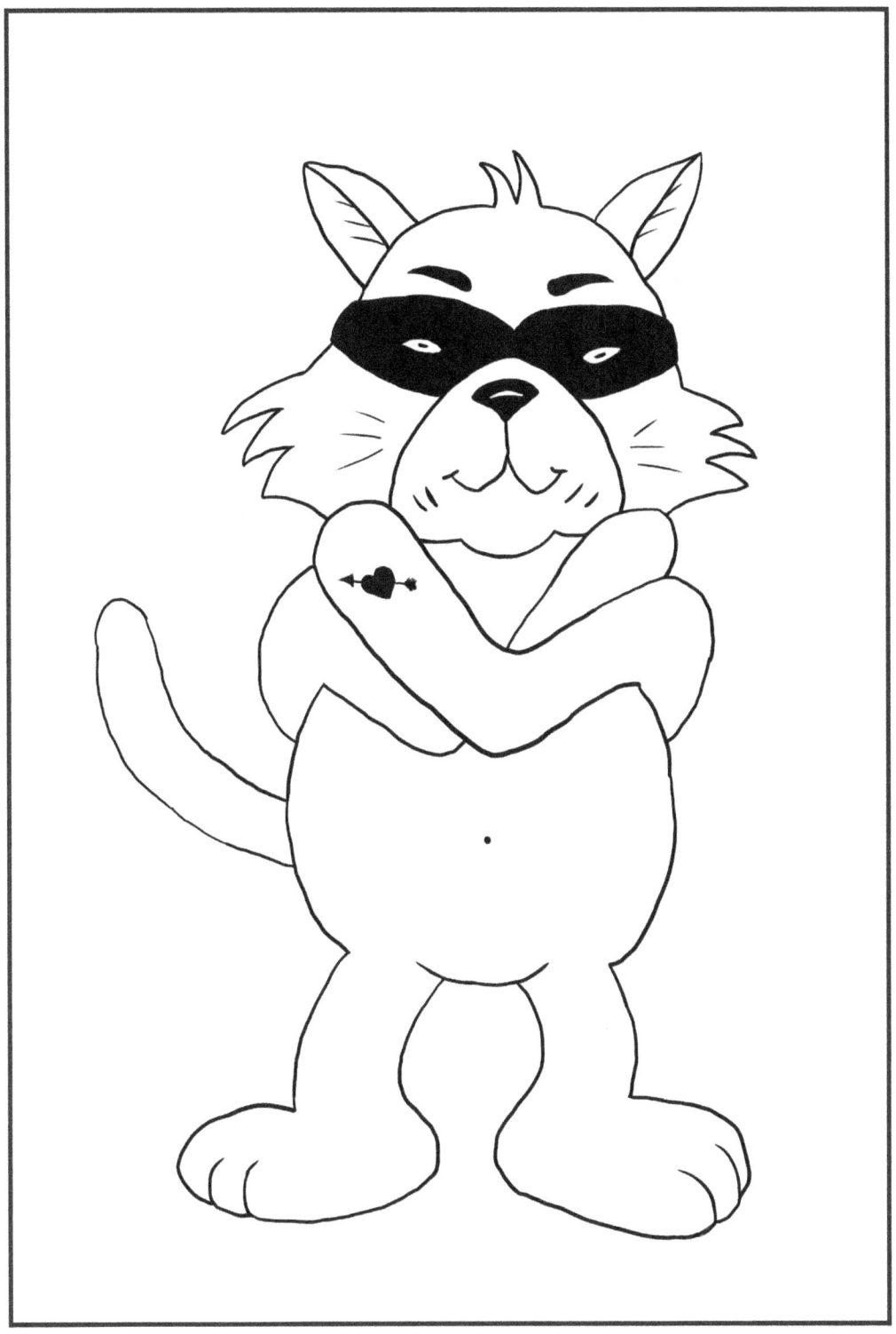

COPYRIGHT NOTIFICATION

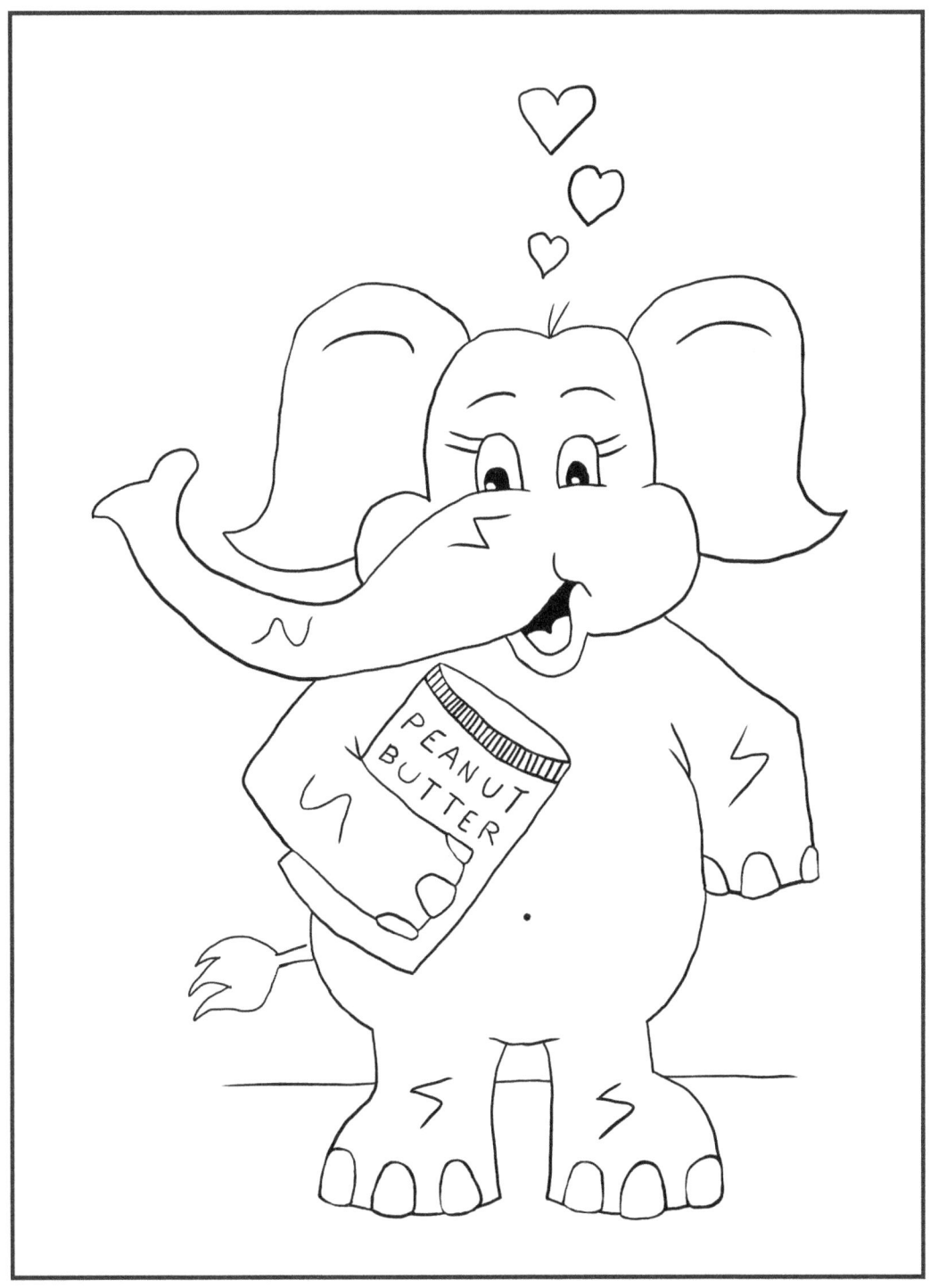

WHAT YOU'LL NEED

- Scrap paper to practice drawing

- A regular graphite pencil

- An eraser

- Pen for inking your sketch (optional)

- Colored pencils (optional)

HOW TO USE THIS BOOK

1. Pick one of the prompts you'd like to draw. If you're stuck, Pinterest is a great site for ideas and inspiration.

2. Next, grab your pencil and some scrap paper. Warm up by creating a few practice sketches.

3. Once you're ready, start drawing your masterpiece. Sketch lightly at first. This will make it easier to fix mistakes.

4. After the basic shapes are drawn, erase unwanted lines and add details like whiskers, stipes or spots.

5. **For pencil artists**: Use shading to create the finished product.

6. **For cartoonists**: You can darken the pencil lines with a pen. **Keeping a piece of *scrap paper under your drawing will prevent the ink from bleeding onto the next page.***

7. *Once the ink is dry, use your eraser and remove any stray pencil marks.*

* Colored pencils can be used to make your drawing stand out.

Draw a goldfish.

Draw a spider in a web.

Draw a caterpillar.

Draw an owl.

Draw a duckling.

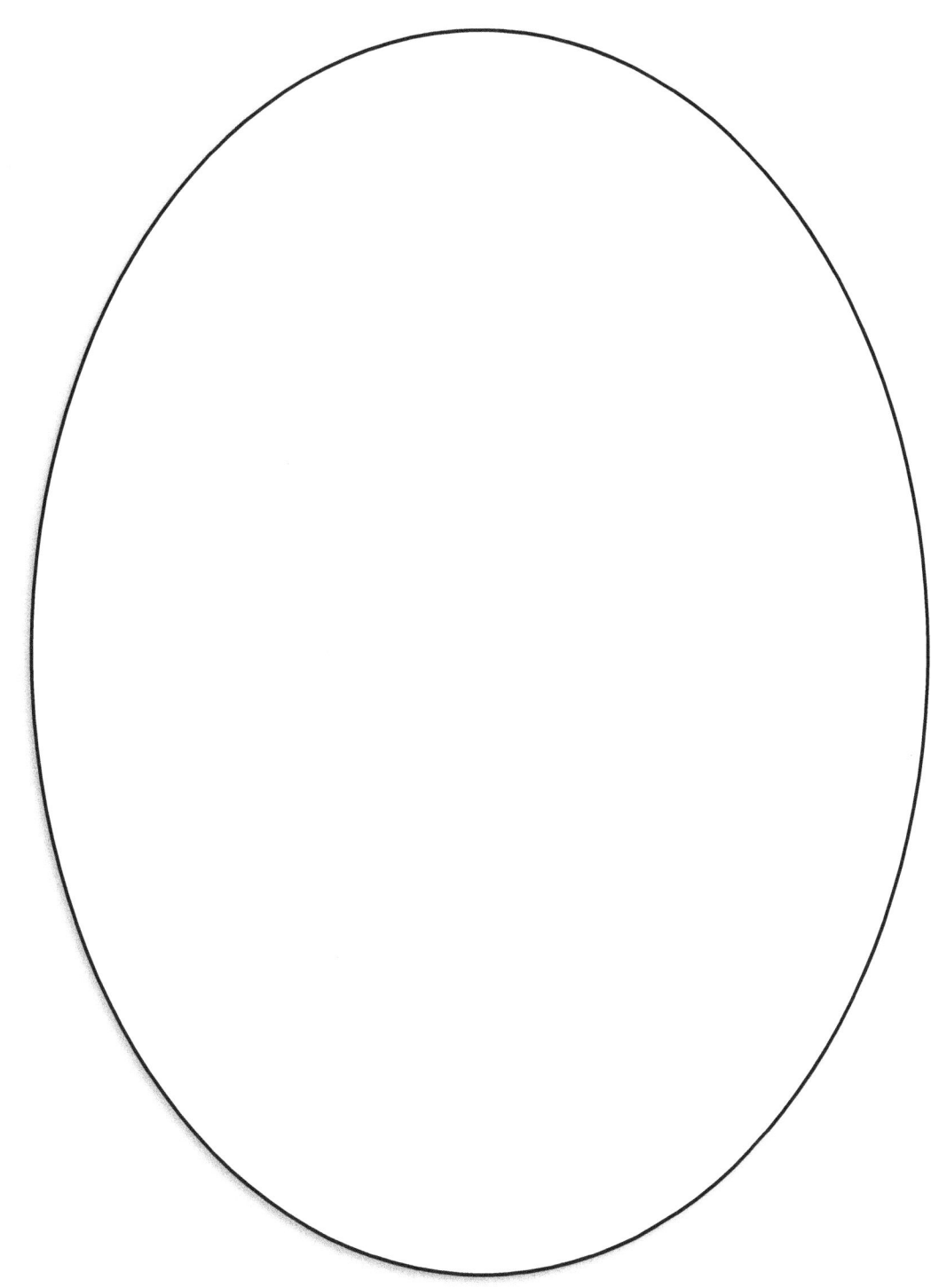

Draw an ant.

Draw a deer.

100 Drawing Prompts for Animal Lovers

Draw a dragonfly.

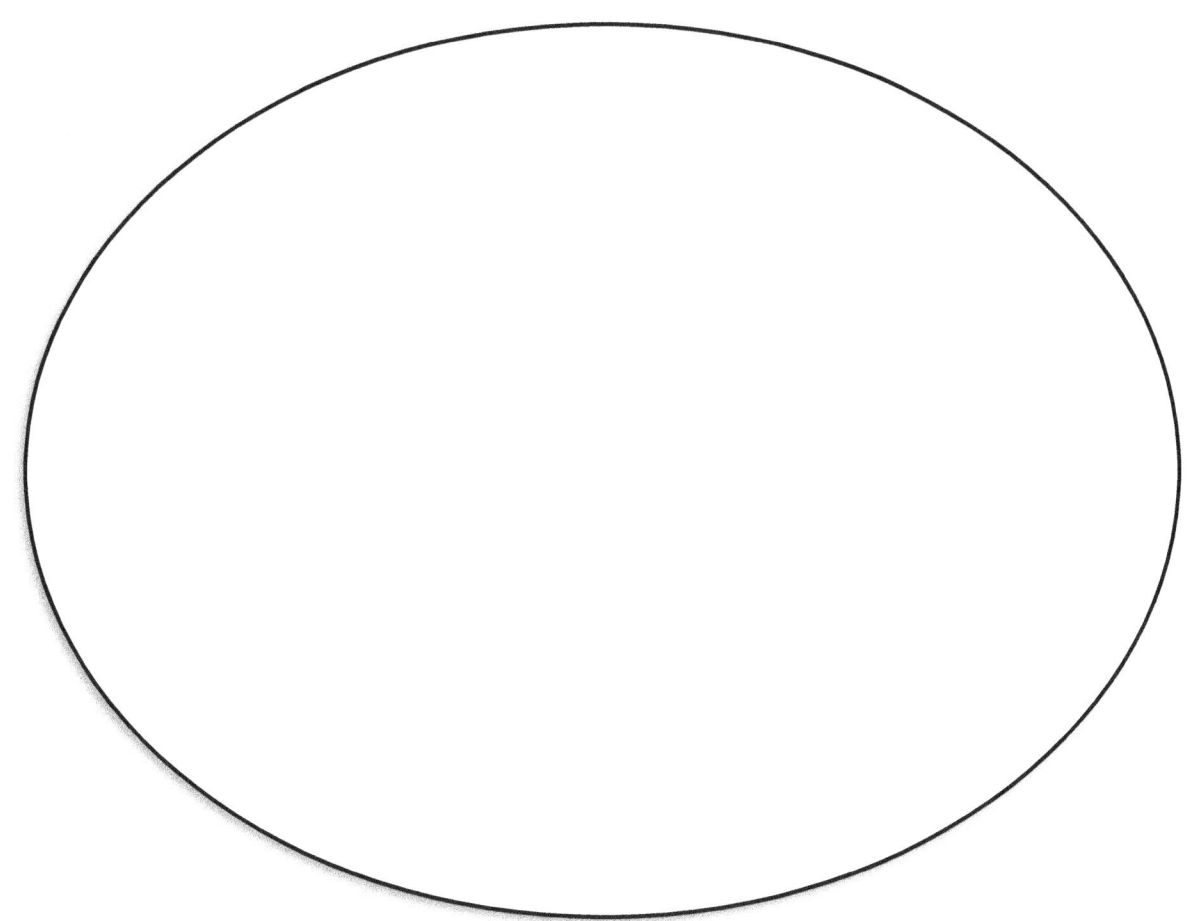

Draw a puppy.

Draw a moose.

Draw a scorpion.

Draw a butterfly.

Draw a hippo.

Draw a calico cat.

Draw a chihuahua.

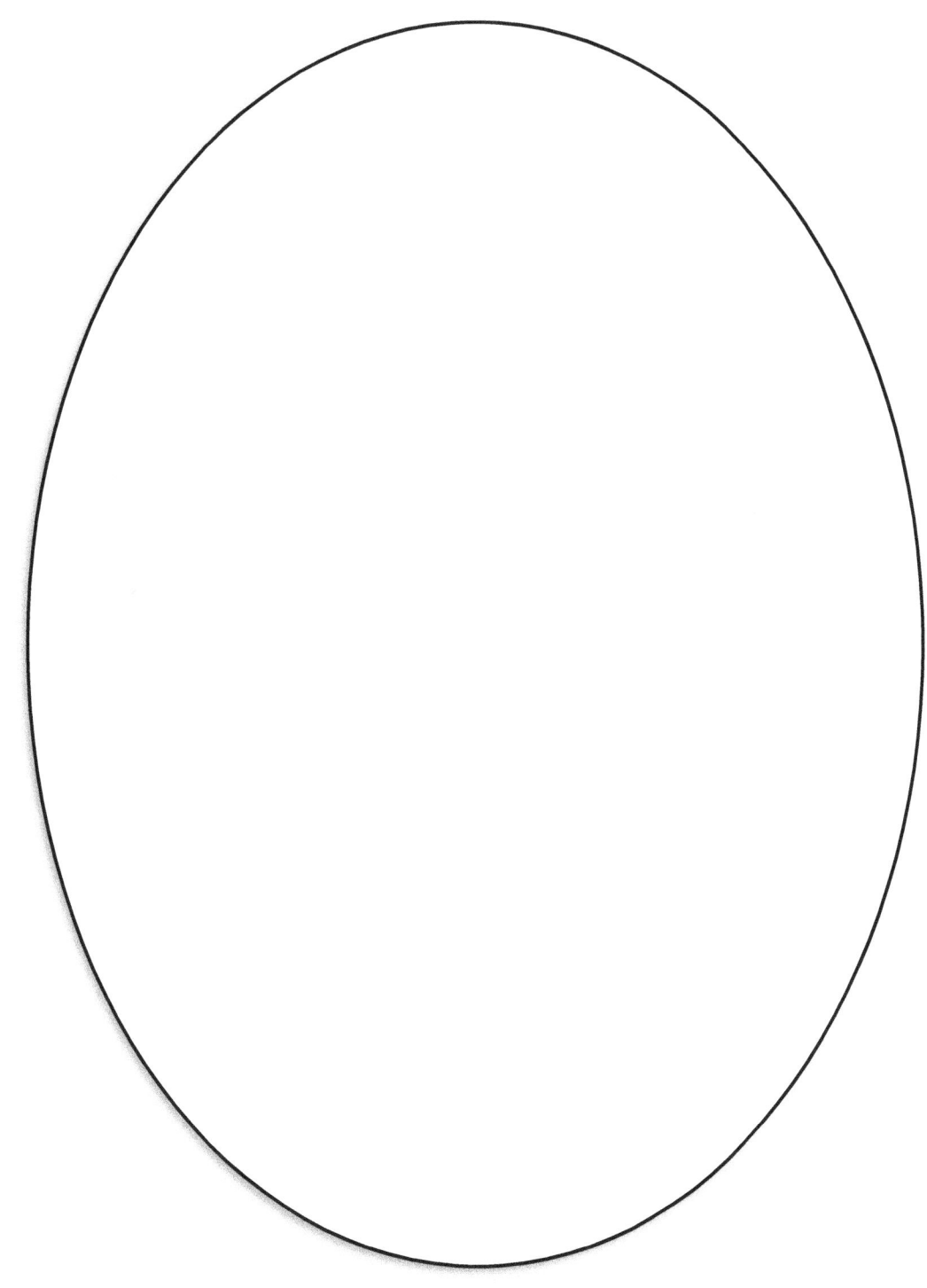

Draw a cow.

Draw a giraffe.

Draw a lion's head.

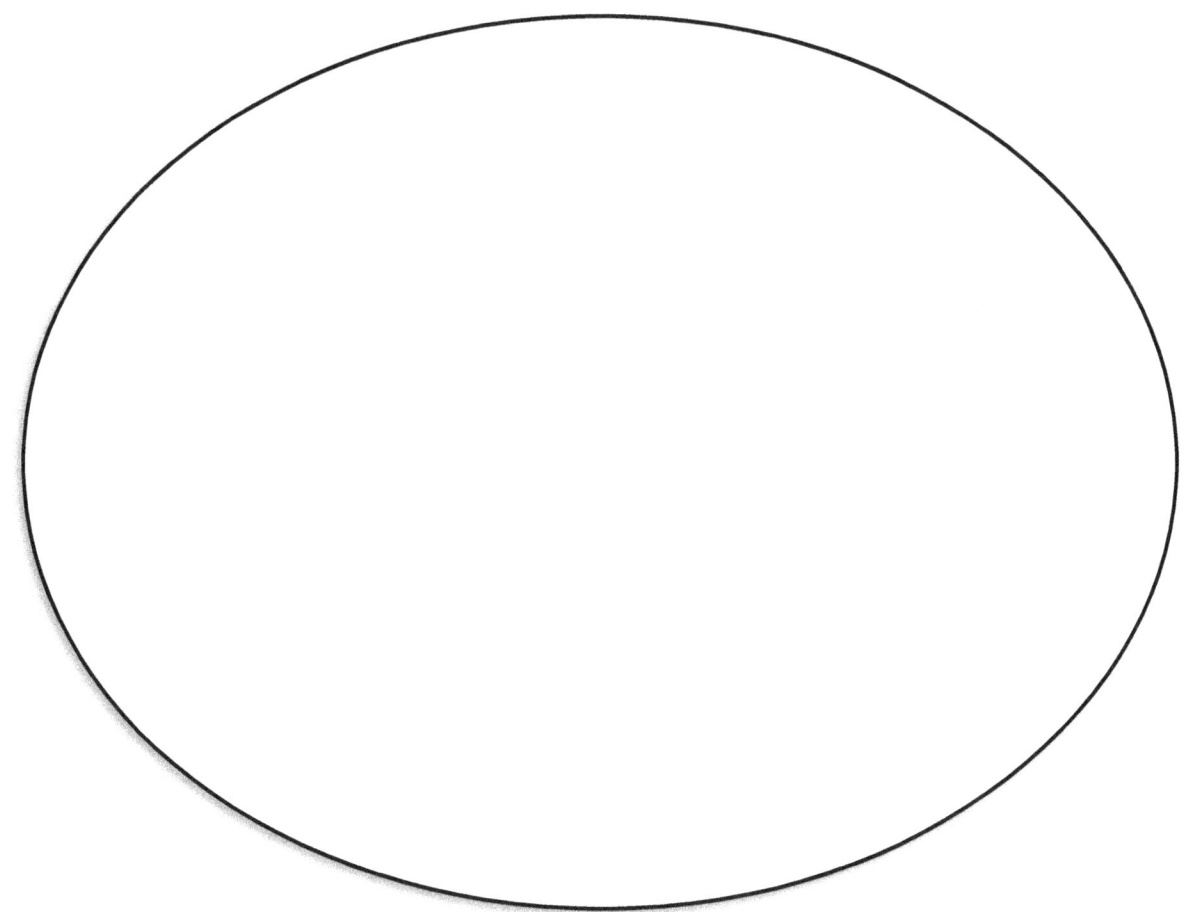

Draw a sheepdog.

45

Draw a grizzly bear on its hind feet.

100 Drawing Prompts for Animal Lovers

Draw a snail.

Draw an eagle.

Draw an elephant.

Draw a fly.

Draw a walrus.

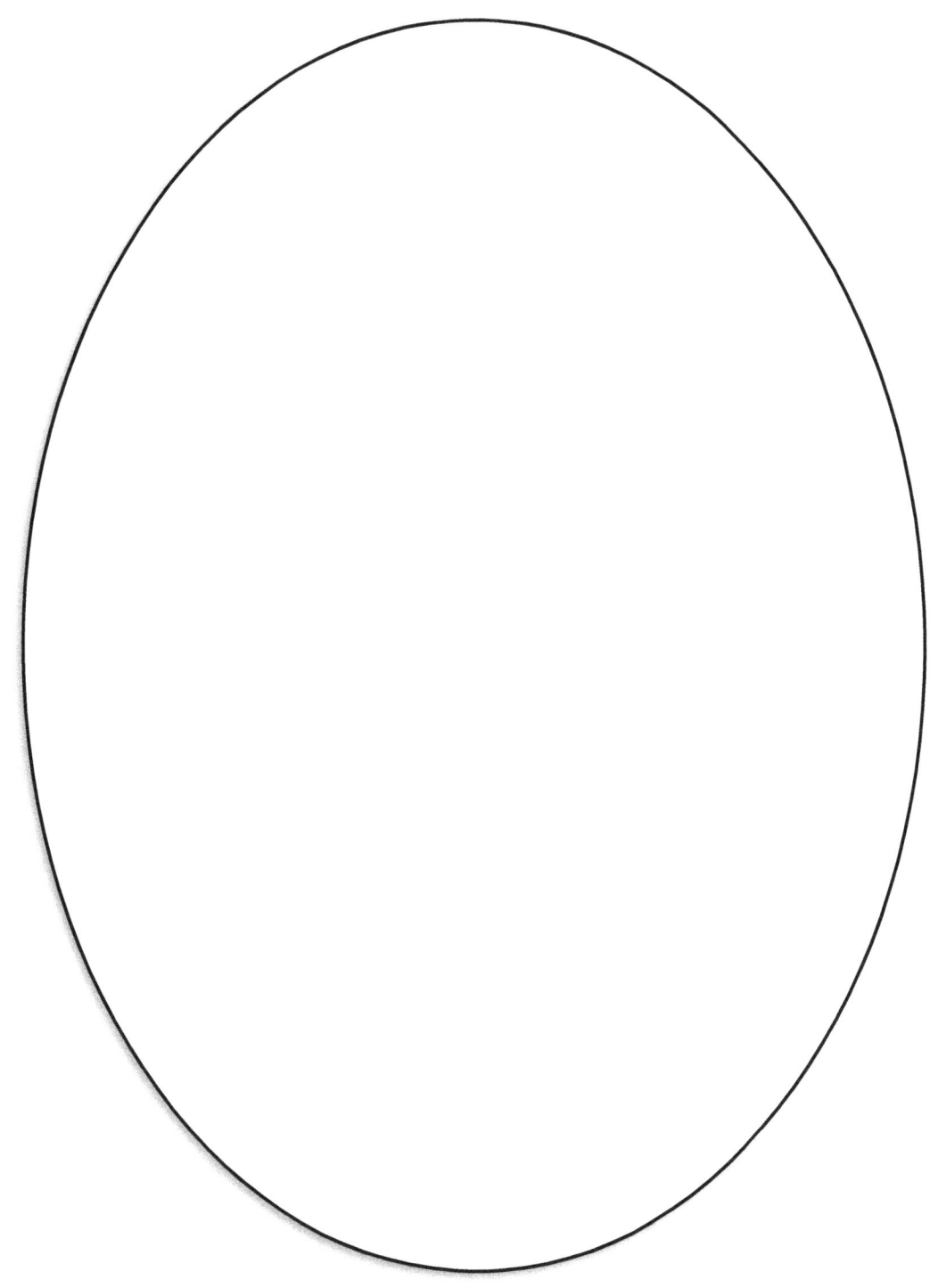

Draw a sword fish.

Draw a Siamese cat.

Draw a bat.

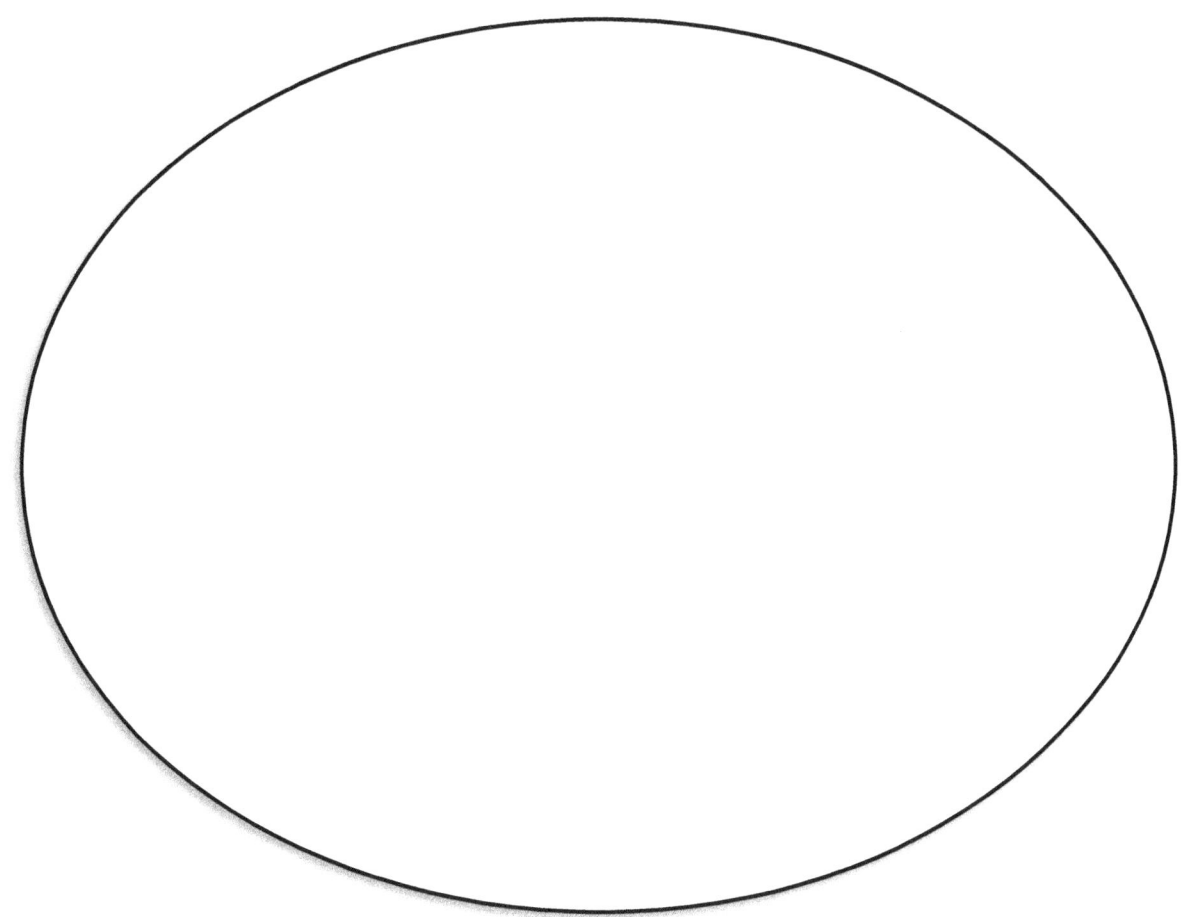

Draw a penguin.

Draw a whale.

Draw a crab.

Draw a bumblebee.

Draw a horse.

73

100 Drawing Prompts for Animal Lovers

Draw a fish jumping from the water.

Draw a seal.

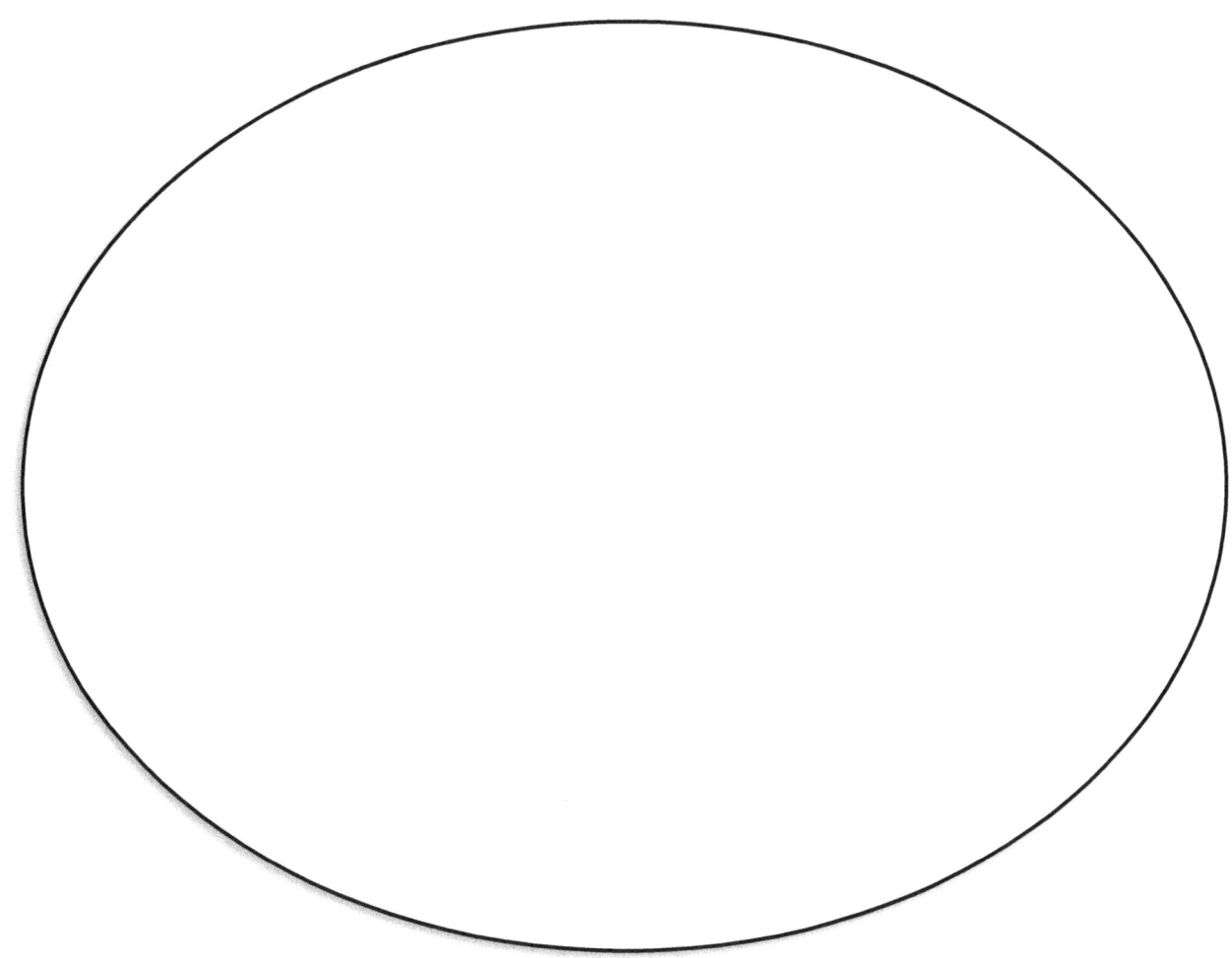

Draw a pig.

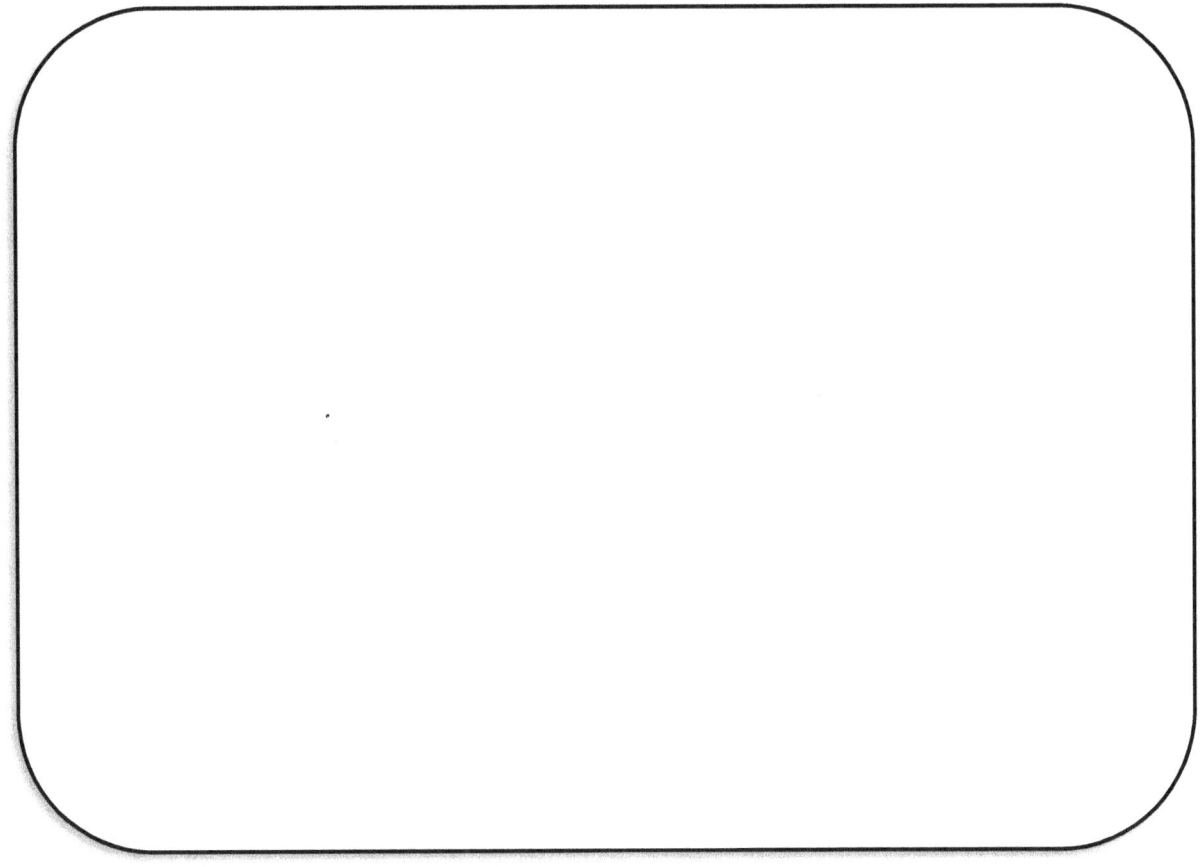

Draw a pelican.

Draw a peacock.

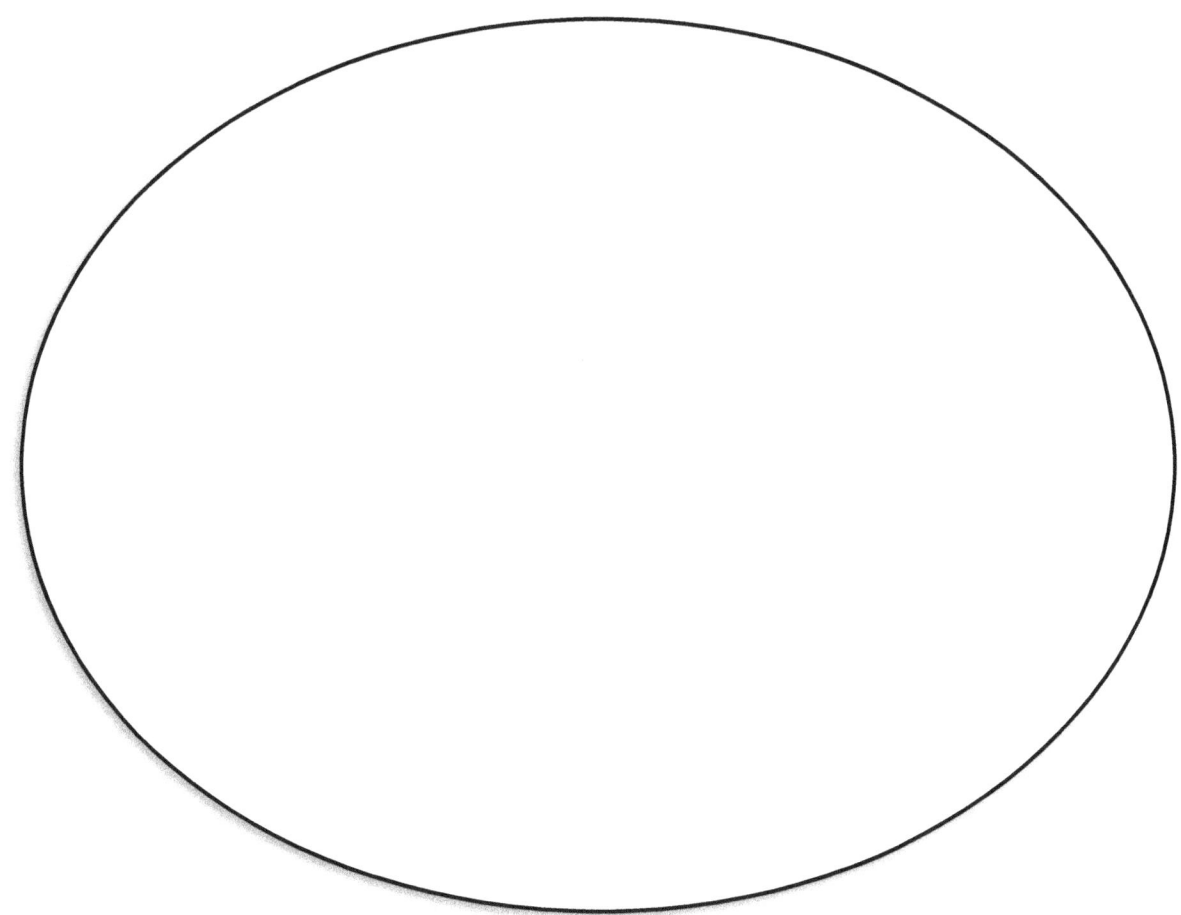

Draw an inch worm.

Draw a squirrel.

Draw a sea turtle swimming in the water.

Draw a hummingbird.

Draw an alligator.

Draw a hamster.

Draw a chipmunk.

100 Drawing Prompts for Animal Lovers

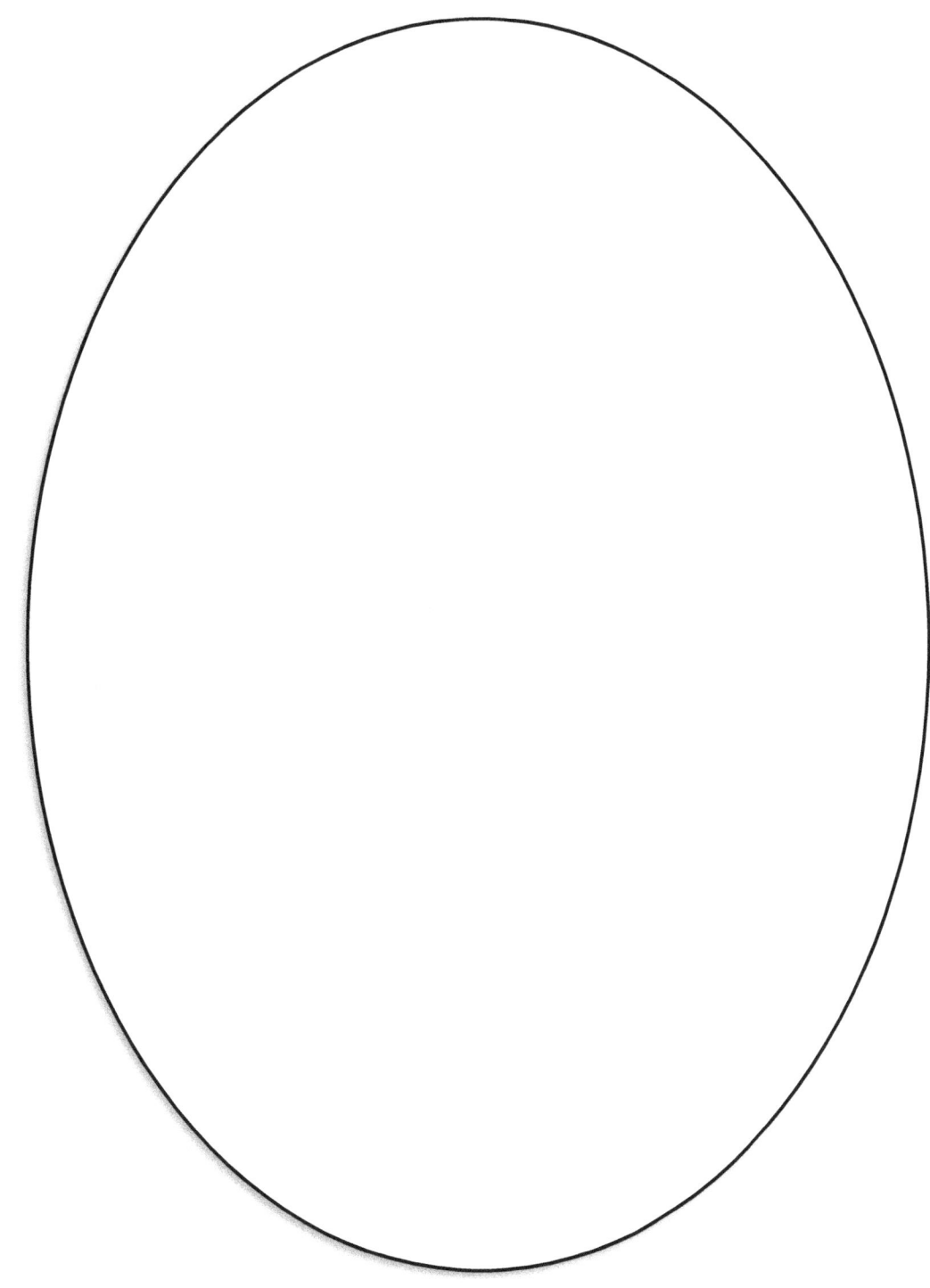

Draw a goat.

Draw a monkey.

Draw a tiger.

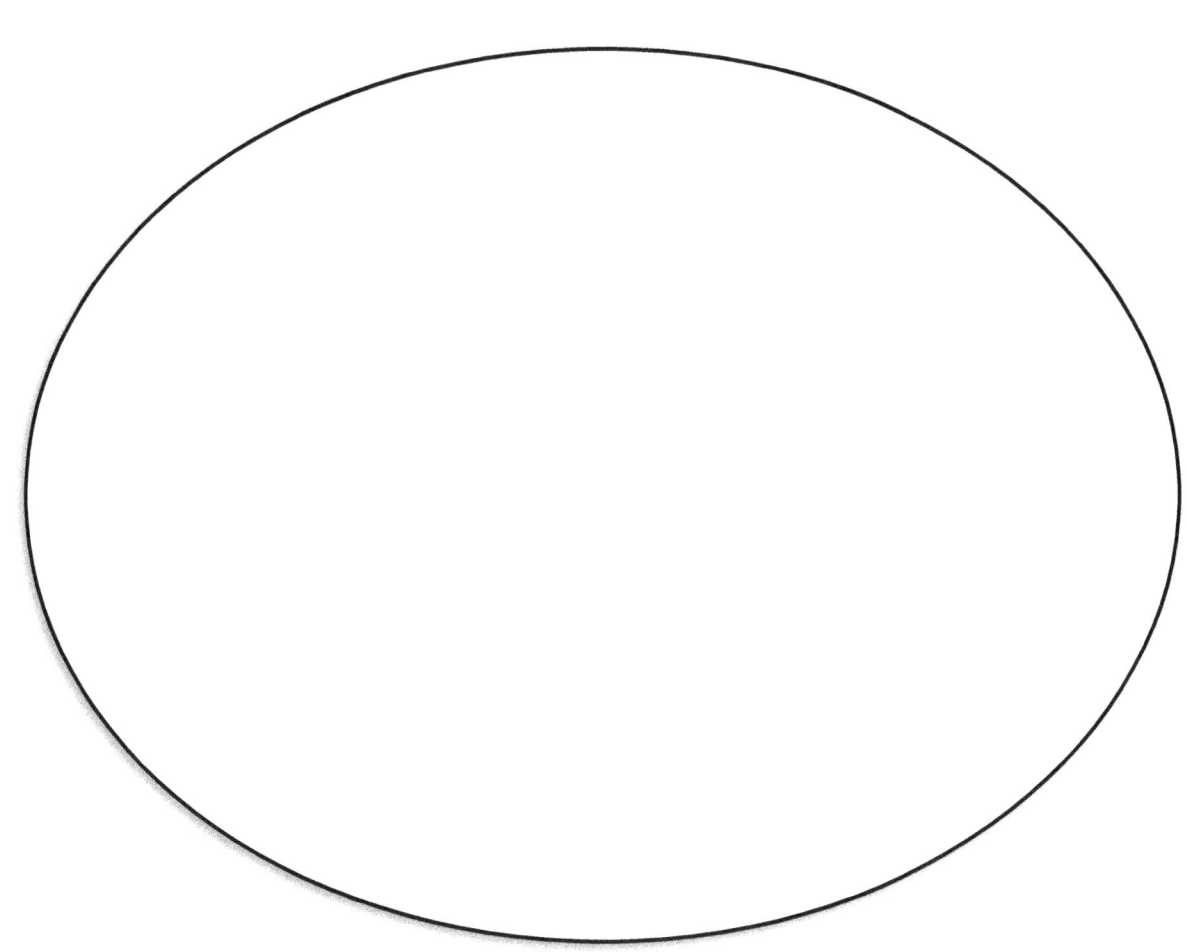

Draw a fox.

Draw a koala bear.

Draw a tarantella.

Draw a frog.

Draw a snake.

Draw a kitten.

Draw a unicorn.

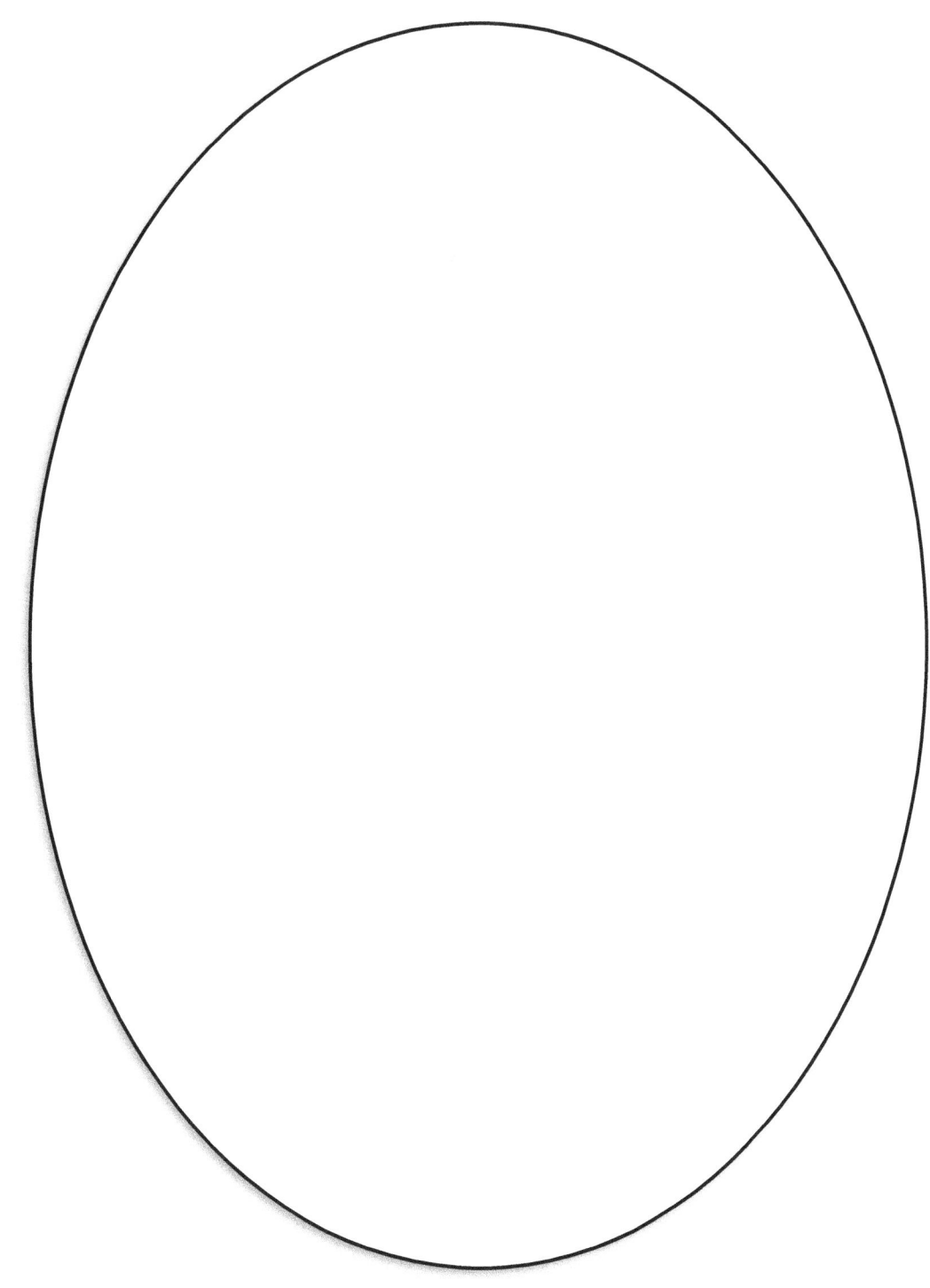

Draw a polar bear.

Draw a gorilla.

Draw a cockatiel.

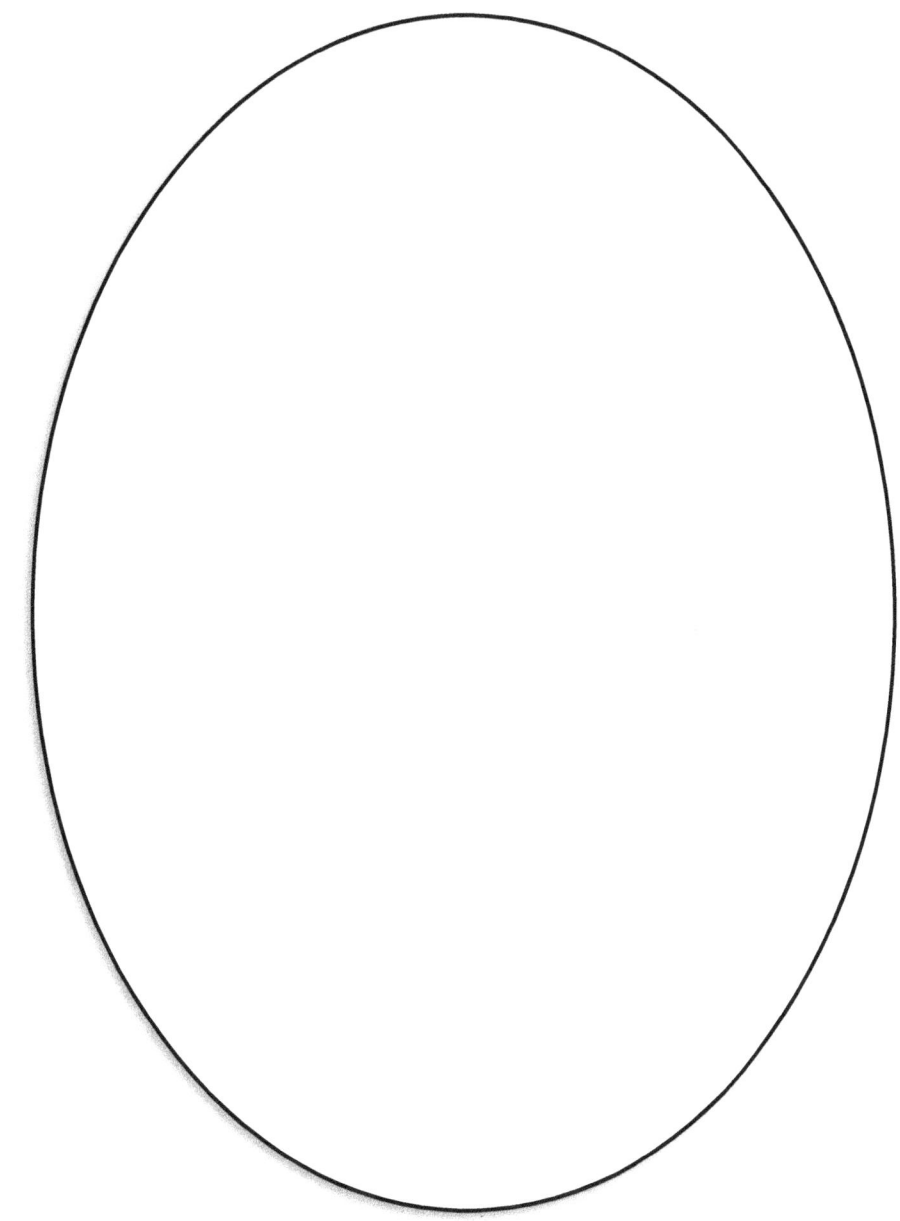

Draw a swan.

100 Drawing Prompts for Animal Lovers

Draw a lop-eared rabbit on it's hind feet.

Draw a lobster.

Draw a panda.

Draw a husky.

Draw a bird in a nest.

Draw a Labrador retriever.

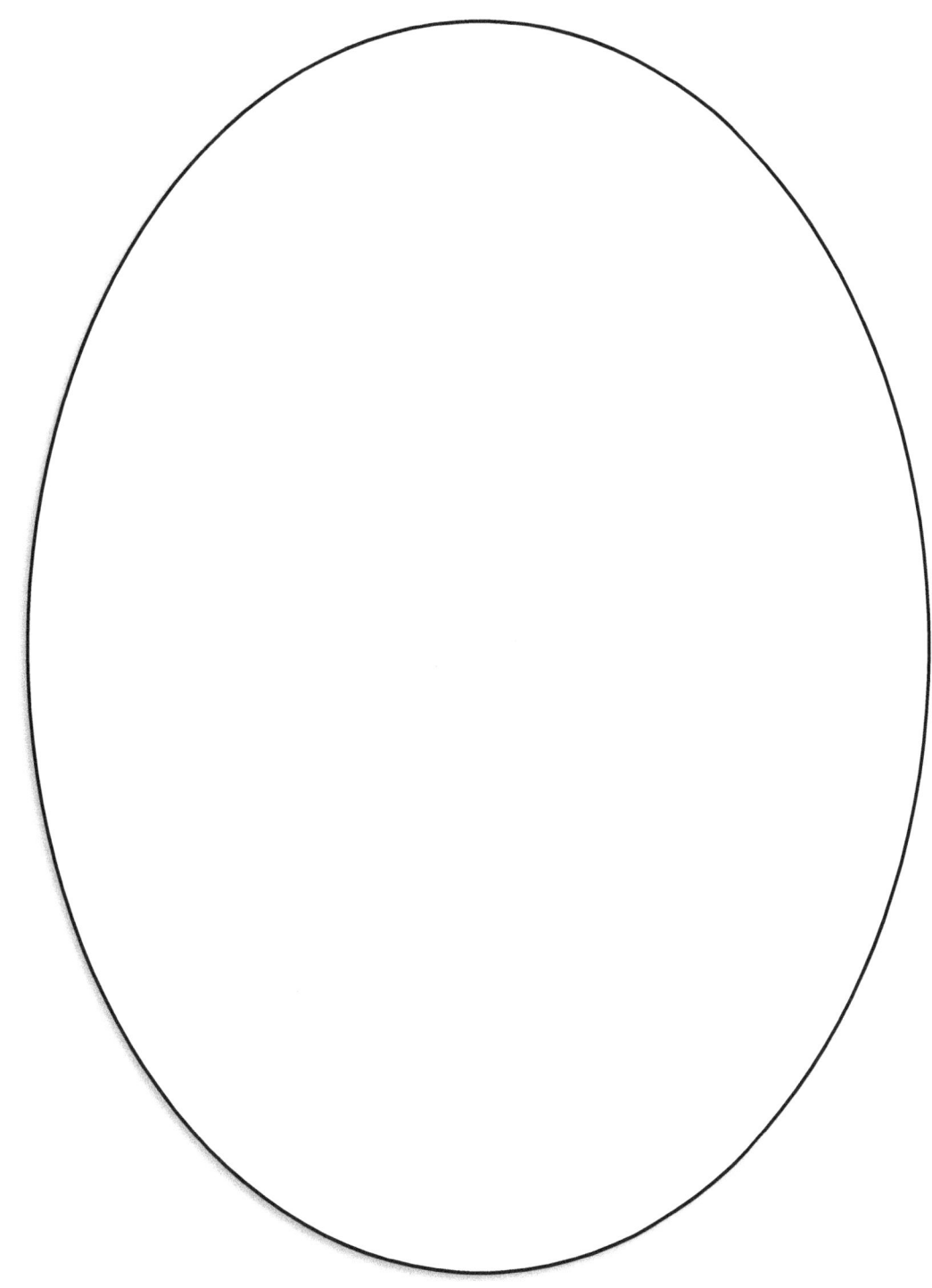

Draw a bulldog.

Draw a kangaroo.

Draw a ladybug.

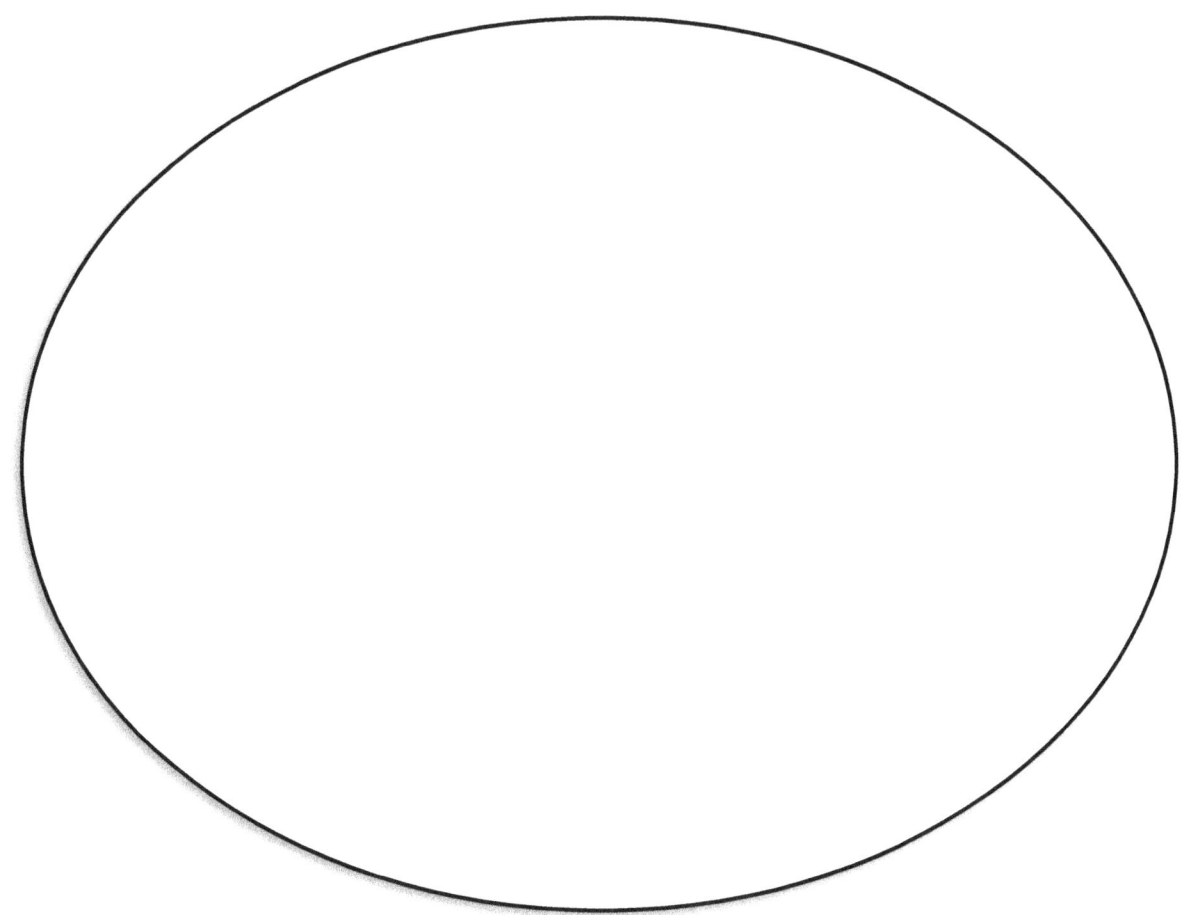

Draw an ostrich.

Draw a beagle.

Draw a starfish.

Draw a coy fish.

Draw a lizard.

Draw a seagull flying in the sky.

Draw a monkey hanging from a tree branch.

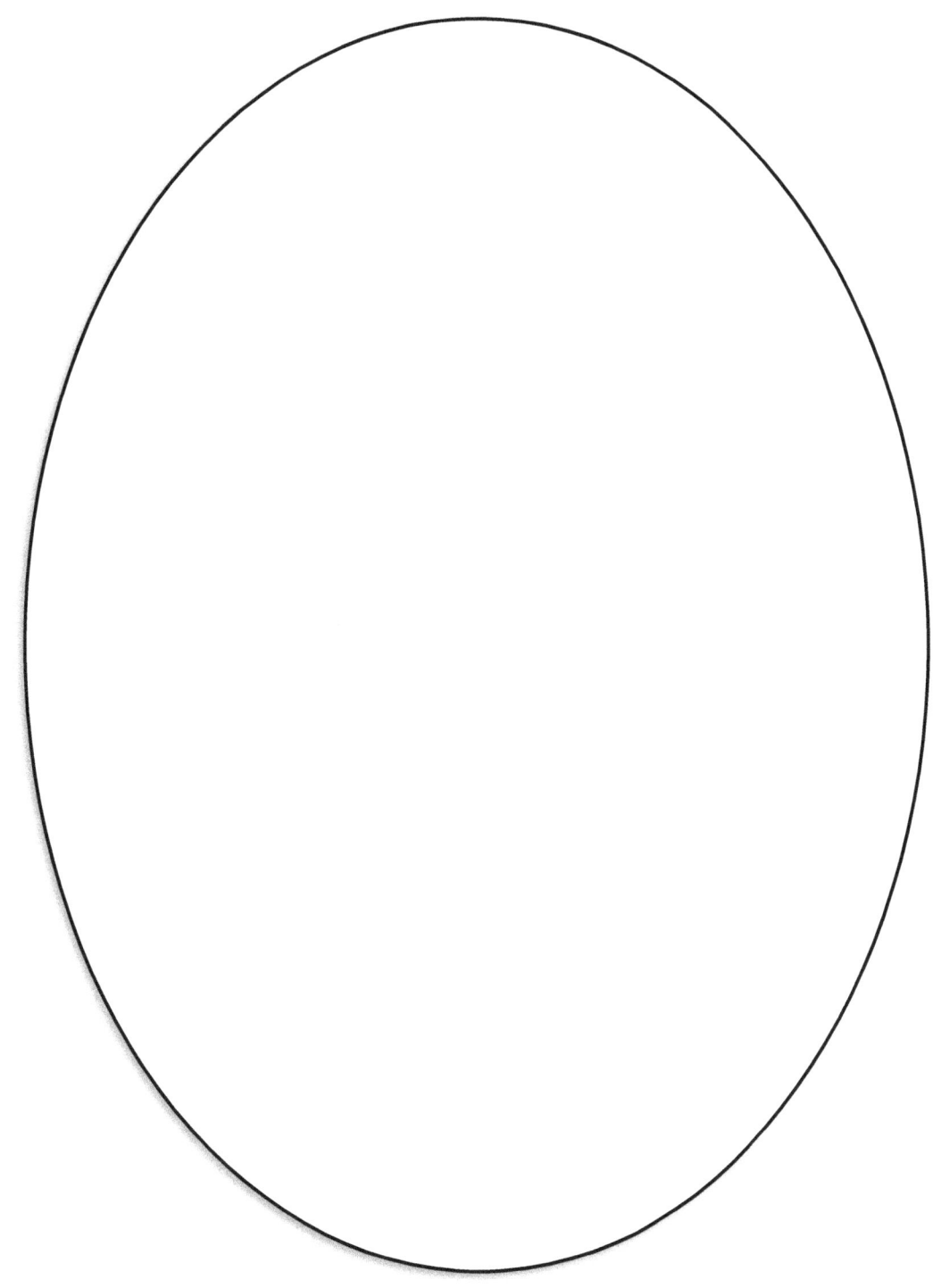

Draw a turtle.

Draw a rooster.

Draw a clam.

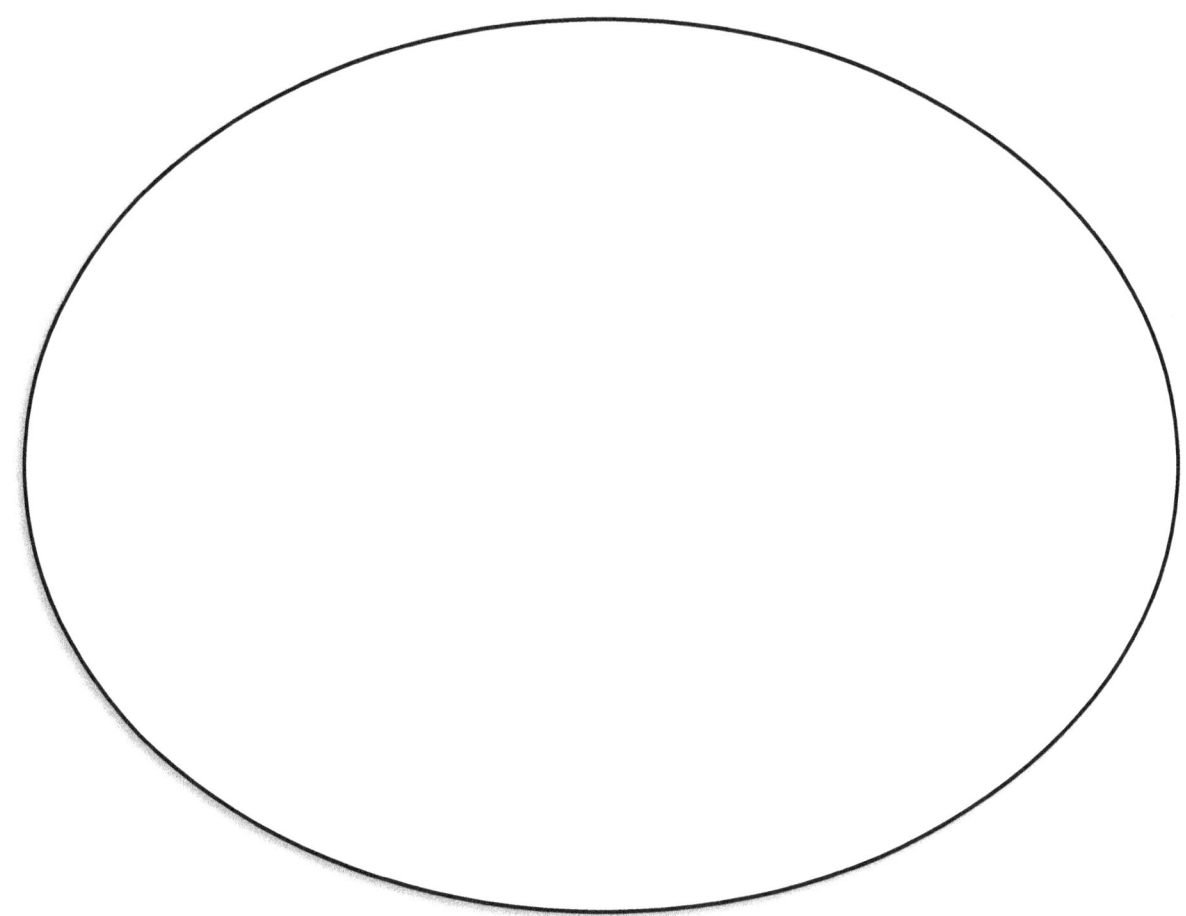

Draw a racoon.

Draw a squid.

Draw a camel.

100 Drawing Prompts for Animal Lovers

Draw a jellyfish.

Draw a mouse.

100 Drawing Prompts for Animal Lovers

174

Draw an octopus.

Draw a swimming eel.

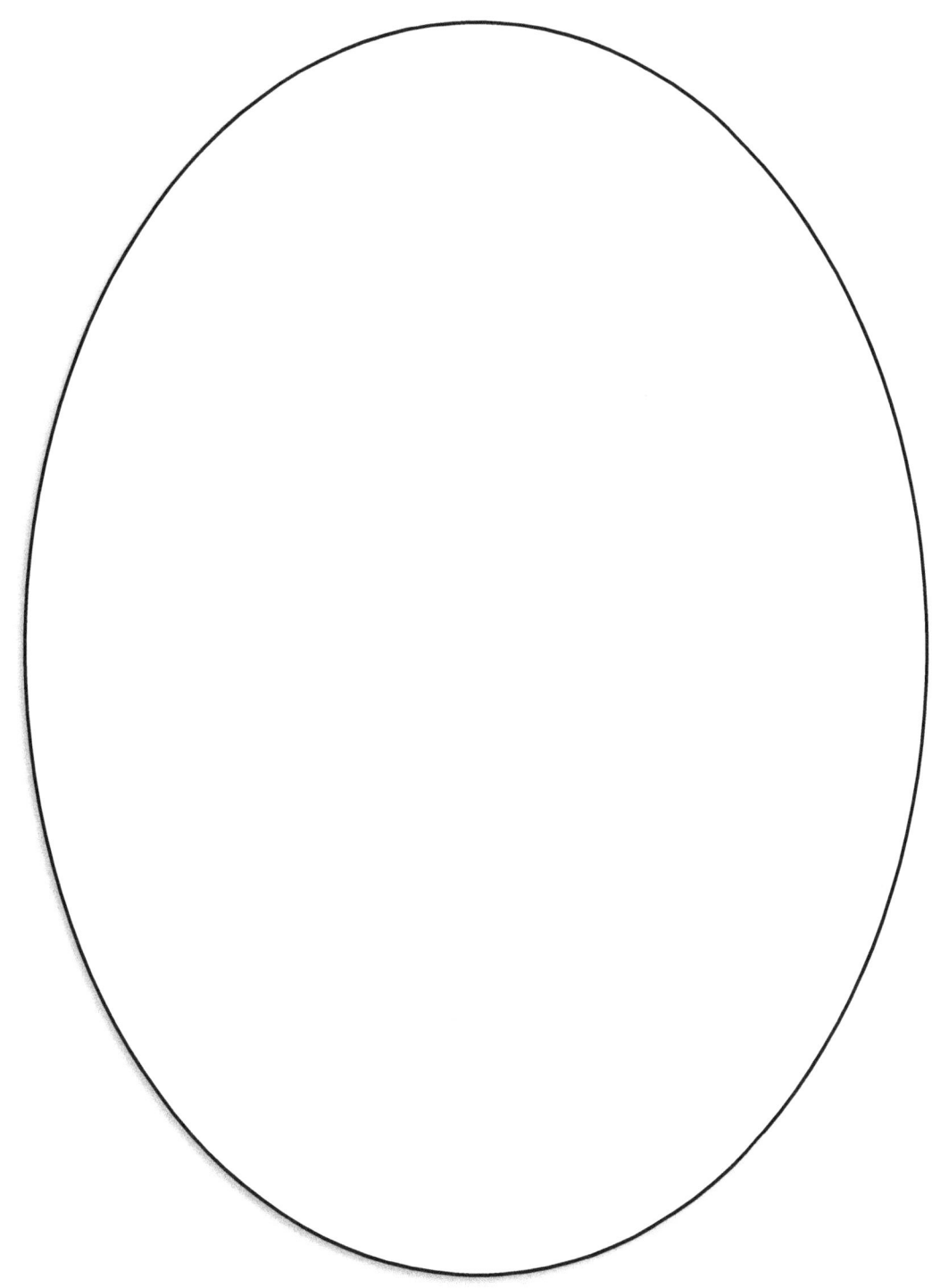

Draw a zebra.

Draw a skunk on his hind legs.

Draw a goose.

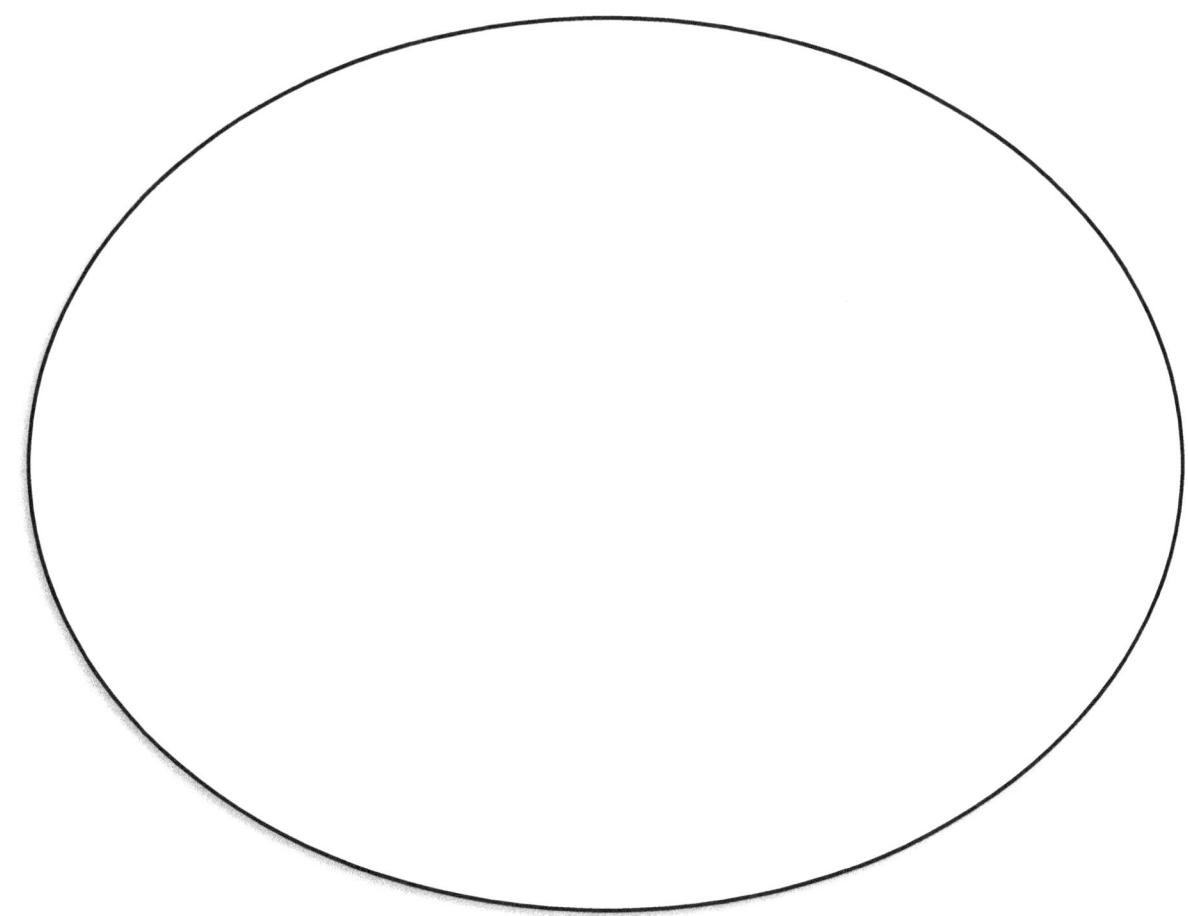

Draw a stingray.

Draw a toucan.

Draw a turkey.

Draw someone's pet.

Draw a dinosaur.

Draw a leopard.

Draw a parakeet.

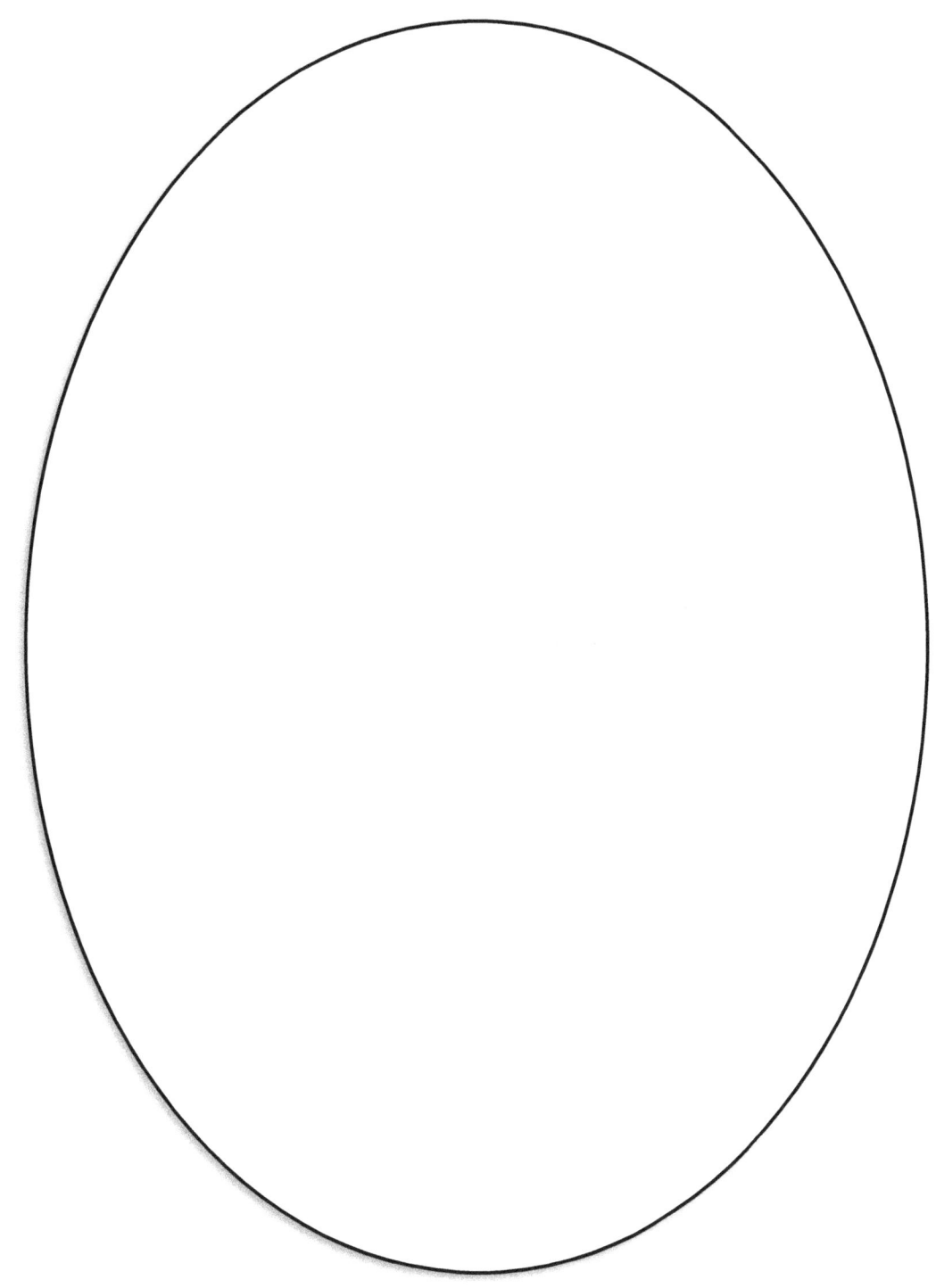

Draw a lamb.

Draw a bug from your imagination.

Draw a shark.

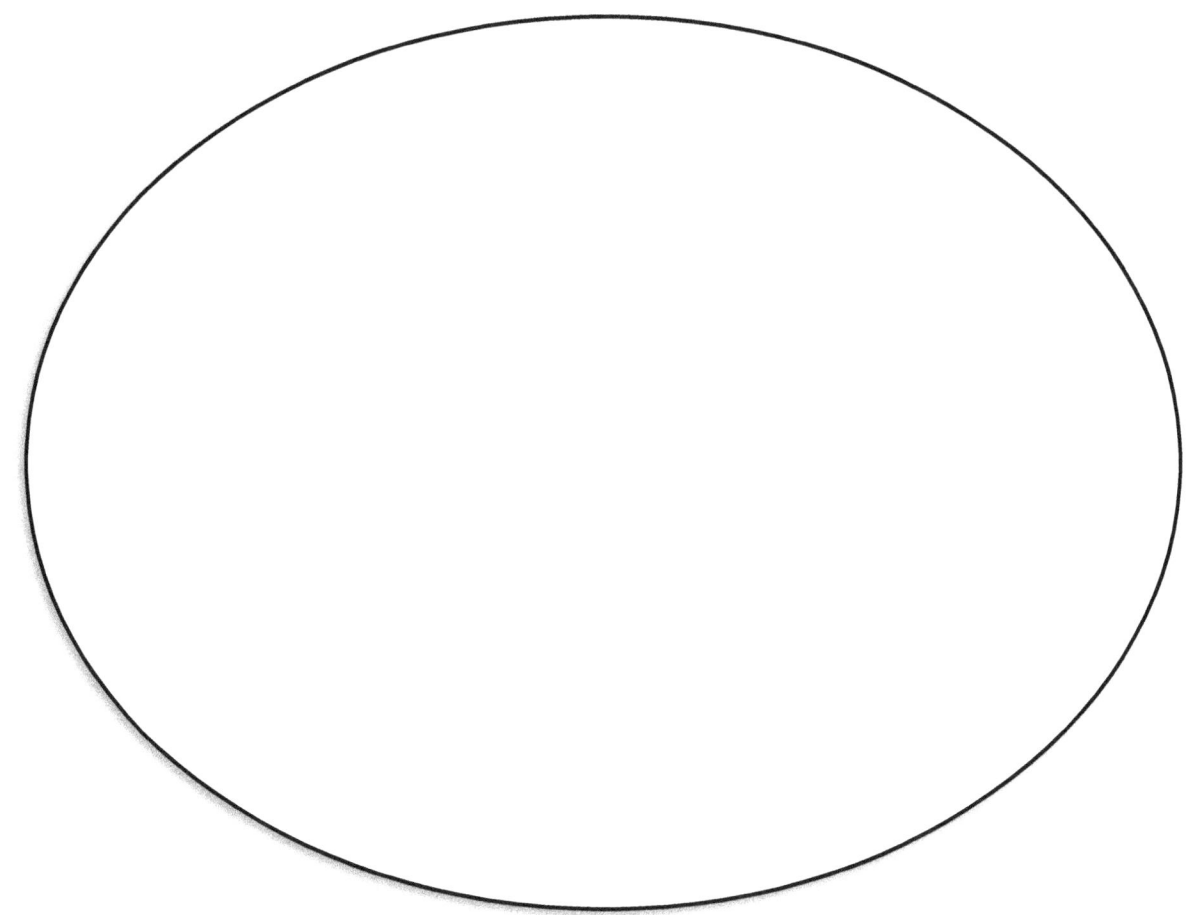

Draw a seahorse.

Draw a macaw.

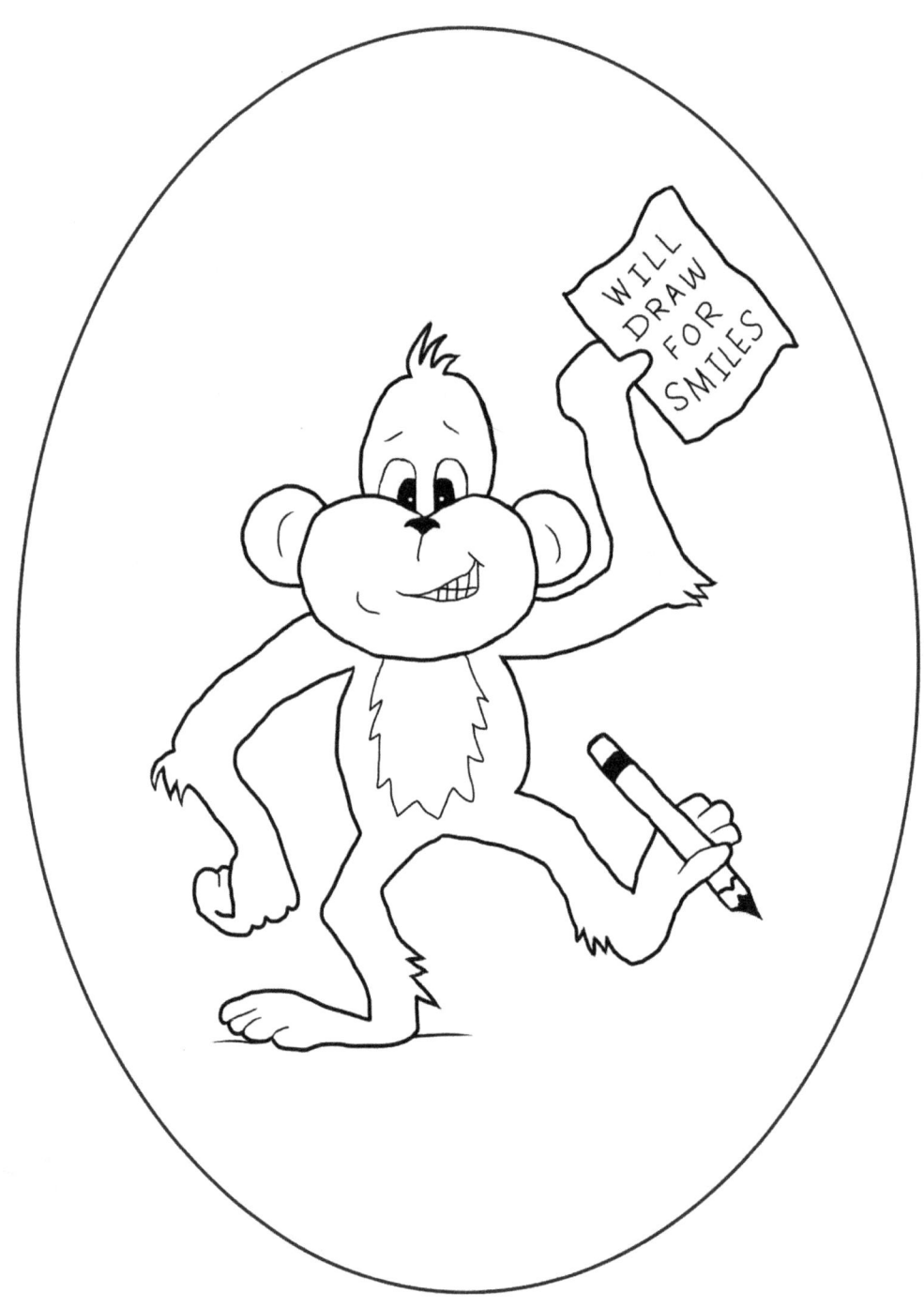

"Bye for now."

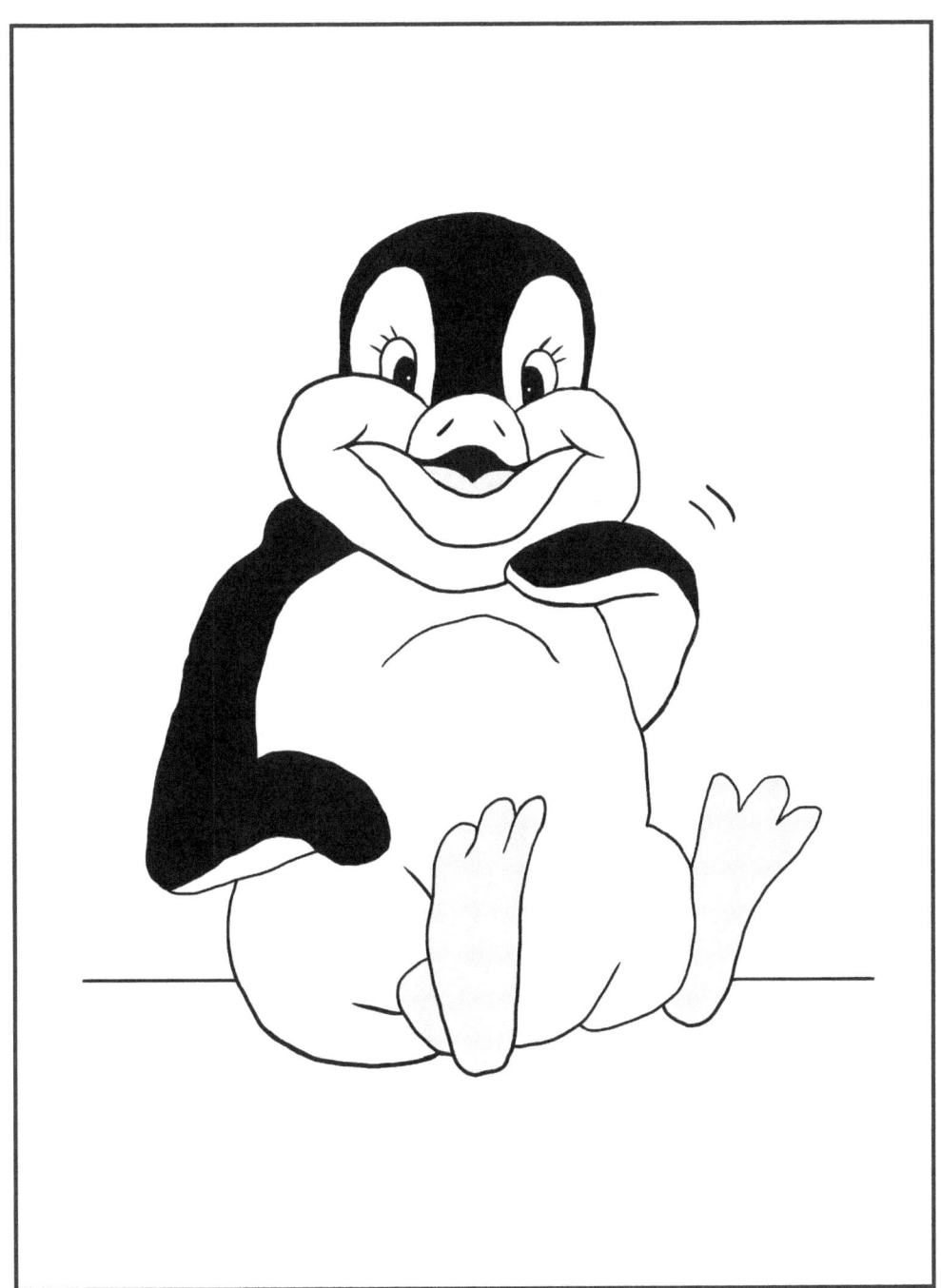

THANK YOU

www.ingramcontent.com/pod-product-compliance
Lightning Source LLC
Chambersburg PA
CBHW080957170526
45158CB00010B/2828